The Write Analysis

Understanding People
Through Their Handwriting

Angela Spencer-Harper

With Best Wishes
from Angela
October 2002

D1275388

Published by
Robert Boyd Publications
260 Colwell Drive, Witney
Oxfordshire OX8 7LW

First published 2000

ISBN: 1 899536 51 5

By the same author

Dipping into the Wells:
The story of the two Chiltern Villages
of Stoke Row and Highmoor
seen through the memories of their inhabitants

Printed and bound by The Alden Group, London and Northampton

The Write Analysis

Understanding People through their Handwriting

To my three grandsons,

Milo, Quentin and Gabriel,

who may find this book useful

to them sometime in the future

Introduction

I first took an interest in Graphology, the science of understanding people through their handwriting, about 40 years ago, when I was browsing in a second-hand bookshop and found a book by an American, Nadya Olyanova, entitled *The Psychology of Handwriting.* Even as I glanced through its pages I could tell that this could be a very useful tool which might help me in many ways.

I later realised it was quite an advanced work for a beginner, so I borrowed more simple books from the local library and then, as and when I came across them, I bought more advanced books, all seeming to put the same laws across, but in a different way.

After a year of reading, I began to do my own analyses, just for my own interest and started to collect letters and other documents, but only from people I knew quite well. In the end I decided that I must have been with the writer for at least an hour before I could make comments on their writing from what I had learned about graphology and from superficial judgements that I could make myself. In this way I began to marry the two together and never found them to be incorrect.

Gradually I built up three lever arch files on correspondence from Family, Friends and Colleagues. Each of them had a slip of paper attached to them, with notes on the handwriting and on the characteristics known to me and, sure enough, they all matched.

From this stage I went on to observe constantly and to list the basic rules for myself. Eventually I was asked to lecture to my local Women's Institute on the subject and went on to give talks to other organisations, Rotary Clubs, Inner Wheel, Townswomen's Guilds, etc.

About twenty years ago I was invited to lecture on Graphology on the Cunard liner, *Queen Elizabeth 2,* affectionately known as the QE2. Here I taught passengers the elementary rules and showed them the many uses of this science and continued to do so for about fifteen years.

In more recent years I have given talks on other cruise ships as well, and it was the Cruise Director of Fred. Olsen ship, *The Black Watch,* Ronnie Finch, who suggested I write this book, to enable lay people to learn the principles of Graphology, from where they can just apply them at a basic level or go on to study the subject further.

I hope this book will inspire you to do just that.

Angela Spencer-Harper
Witheridge Hill
Henley-on-Thames

January 2000

With permission of the Parker Pen Company

Handwriting Analysis

The Science of Graphology

Graphology is sometimes thought of as a parlour game, rather like *Consequences*, a bit of fun. In fact it is, as the 'ology' part of its name implies, a science with rules which, once mastered and understood, can give even a lay person a very useful tool with which to begin to understand people and sometimes see other qualities in someone they thought they knew so well.

Graphology goes back to Roman times and is based on the Greek words *graphos*, which means marks made by movements of the hand, dictated by the brain, and *logos*, meaning word. I say hand movements, but even in people who have to use their foot or mouth as a means of controlling the pen or brush, the basics of their character are still obvious to the trained eye. It enables you to have an insight into the writer and though for serious purposes it is necessary to have several lengthy documents for analysis, even a brief note on a greetings card will indicate basic traits.

The value of this science often lies, not only in interpreting the writing of persons known to you, your friends, family, neighbours and colleagues, but will also enable you to form some impression of a person that you have never met. What will soon become surprising to you is the extent to which handwritings do vary and soon you will not only be able to recognise the familiar penmanship of a friend, but also certain characteristics in letters or documents written by persons unknown to you. This is especially useful in business and that is why graphology is used a great deal in personnel work today, especially in the fields of career guidance and team-building.

It is also useful in learning to get along better with your family and colleagues. You may be able to help someone through a better understanding of them, instead of criticising them in what could prove to be a destructive manner. Graphology enables you to see that there is more to someone than meets the eye, that a businessman may have artistic qualities or a career woman may also be a good home-maker. It is this ability that enables qualified psychologists and graphotherapists to assist their patients through counselling on a range of personal problems.

Of course, it is not possible to make in-depth judgements of people's characters just by reading this book. It is intended only to give an introduction to this science and to show you how you can use it at this level, just as an interest or, if you so wish, then to take your studies further.

At what ever level you do practise this science, don't make sweeping statements based on a little knowledge which, as we know, is always a dangerous thing. Remember to be ever charitable, emphasising the positive side of a person's nature, for instance that they are generous rather than extravagant!

Incidentally, I use the term 'he' throughout this book, but it does, of course, apply equally to women as well as men.

Envelopes

For the lay person, most graphological analyses begin with receiving a letter, so let us start with the envelope in which it is received.

You may or may not recognise the hand as being from someone you know, (presuming it has not been typed!)   However, even then, some of the following rules may still apply.

To be correct, the address should appear in the lower middle of the envelope, leaving sufficient space above it for the postmark not to obliterate the name of the addressee. People who produce envelopes written in this way are usually excellent communicators, have a good sense of planning, are forward thinking and well organised.

On the other hand, if the address is badly written, the writer may have a poor aesthetic sense, not be a very good planner and even lack common sense (because parts of the address may be obliterated by the postmark). Letters like this are often from someone with a poor education.

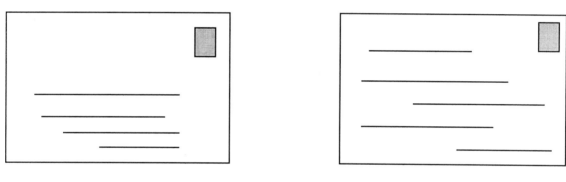

A well-planned envelope   A poorly planned envelope

Then there are those few people who place the address to one side or the other, leaving a great deal of space unused. As you will see in later chapters, this is an indication of either a very shy nature or quite the reverse. People who write to the extreme left tend to be introverted, shy and not readily willing to join in with others. Sometimes, especially where the writing also slants to the left, they are often rather insecure and not good at social contact.

On the other hand, people who place the address to the extreme right, especially if their handwriting also slopes to the right, are those who are forward thinking, sociable characters who may be occasionally impulsive.

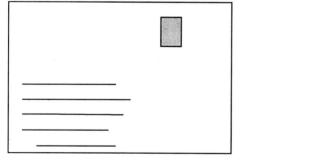
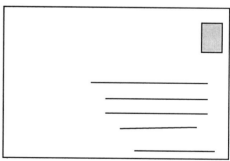

The shy, introverted writer   The forward thinking extrovert

Sometimes the whole address is written at the top of the envelope, or even all at the bottom of it. People who write at the top, can be thought of as not having their feet on the ground, because they do not seem to realise that the franking will make it difficult to read the name of the addressee. However, they are much more 'up in the clouds' than the person who spreads his address out all down the envelope. In fact they are usually dreamers, who give very little thought to what they are actually doing.

The person who writes the whole address very low down on the envelope tends to have an earthy, materialistic nature.

It should be remembered that none of these indications should be read entirely on their own and you will also need to look at other aspects of the writing which will be explained in coming chapters.

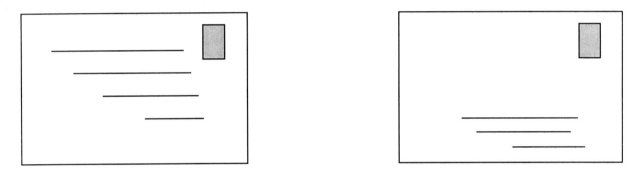

The address placed high up   *The address is placed low down*

Occasionally one receives an envelope where the address occupies almost all the envelope, usually in this case the writing is very large, a sure indication that the writer is a very busy, big thinking person who uses his space and time to the very maximum.

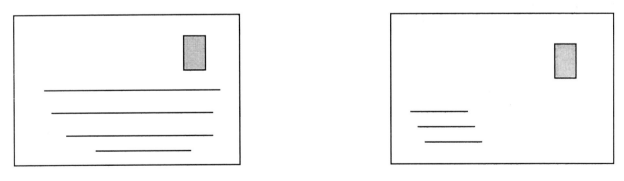

The expansive nature   *The hermit-like nature*

The person with tiny writing, on the other hand, may be happy at home or in a narrow, well known and safe environment.

Margins

As soon as you open the letter, take a note of the margins. These can be quite revealing. A narrow left hand margin indicates someone who is very careful with their money and is not very sociable. They like to stick to what and who they know. Wide left hand margins, on the other hand, show generosity and warmth, especially if there is also a narrower margin to the right, ie the writer tends to think forward. When these are combined with a left slanting or right slanting hand respectively, you can be more sure of these traits.

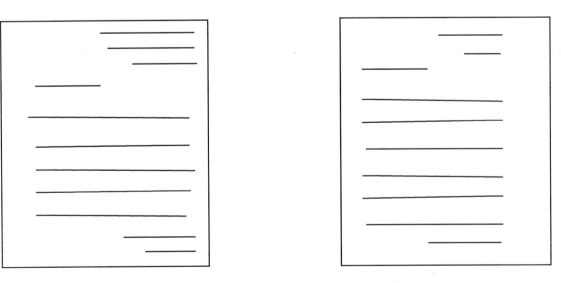

Narrow left margin   *Wide left margin*

A narrow right margin shows the writer is going outwards to meet the person to whom he is writing, he is friendly and sociable. The wide right margin indicates a tendancy to be more insular and less likely to adapt to change.

Narrow right margin   *Wide right margin*

You may receive a letter from someone who has not laid the letter out at all well. They just use the top of the paper, leaving the bottom half blank. This shows lack of forethought and poor planning ability. It is often found in young, inexperienced people or those who have not had a good education. This is especially so where the writing is all at the top of the page. However, the most common is where the writer starts off well but crams more and more in at the bottom of the page, also a sign of lack of foresight - someone who is always in a rush and out of breath!

The poorly planned letter   *The breathless writer*

The writer who uses wide margins on both sides usually has a strong aesthetic sense. They can be quite formal and lovers of tradition, an antiques collector, for example. Such people have usually had a good education, be in a comfortable financial state and are very confident. The last example is of the well-laid out letter with equally spaced margins, which shows clarity of thought, strong self-confidence and a good sense of planning.

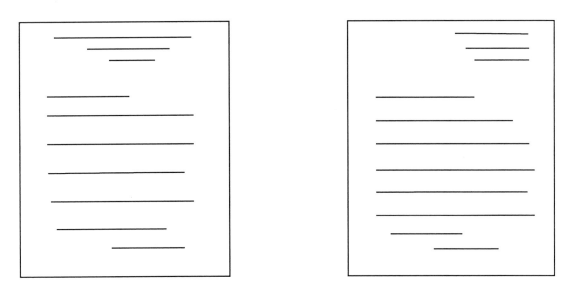

The cultured hand   *The well-laid out letter*

Slope of Lines

The way in which the lines slope is another indication of the kind of person that wrote the letter. Hopefully the document will have been written on unlined paper and if the lines are ruler straight you will be dealing with someone who is very neat and tidy but often rigid in their outlook and unwilling to change. Often the lines of writing are uneven, 'wavy navy' style - this writer is much more adaptable, but may also be unpredictable!

The rigid writer

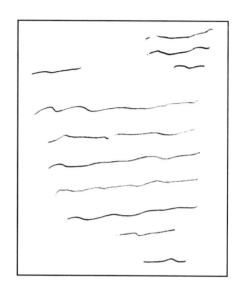

The flexible writer

When the lines slope upwards it is often a sign of an optimistic and cheerful nature. However, it may simply be that the writer is in a good mood, or has just received good news. Every factor must be taken into account with others, for instance, whether the writing always rises or only sometimes. Alternatively the writing may slope downwards. Again, this may mean a pessimistic nature or just a temporary state, such as bereavement, ill health or simply tiredness.

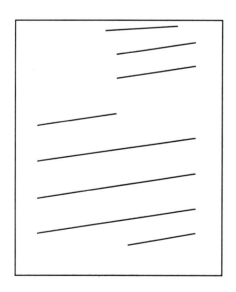

The cheerful writer

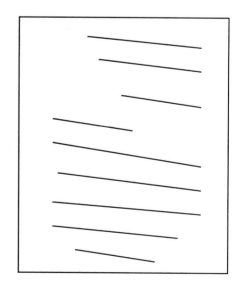

The pessimistic writer

Where the lines are excessively upward sloping, the writer may be unrealistically optimistic, too ambitious and have little sense of reality. Gamblers often have this type of slope - they are always confident that things will be better, whereas quite often they are not improving at all! Sometimes it is a false cheerfulness in face of bad times.

Conversely, very downward sloping lines, fortunately rare, show someone who is very depressed or going through a really bad patch.

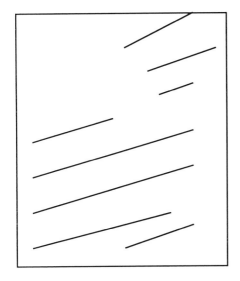

Excessive optimism

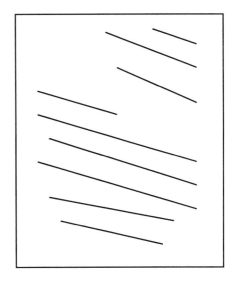

Excessive pessimism

Occasionally you receive a letter from someone who writes in a curved line, either upwards and then downwards or vice-versa. The first type is quite cheerful as he starts to write and is in danger of becoming too much so. Subconsciously, in order to correct this he comes down again - it is a sort of balancing action. The reverse also applies to someone who is in danger of going downwards and so checks himself and goes up again. It may also indicate one who has a lack of staying power, as they cannot maintain the rush of adrelalin needed to keep up the momentum.

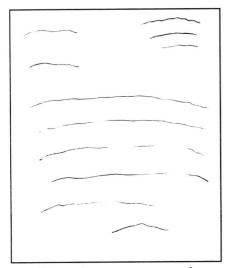

Lines that curve upwards

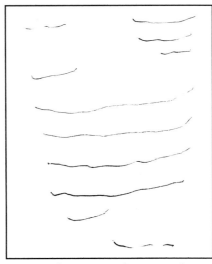

Lines that curve downwards

The Emotional Barometer

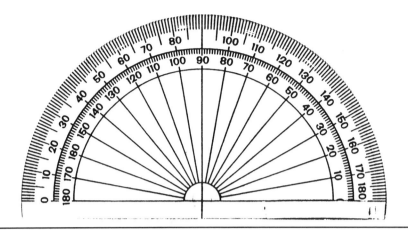

The way in which the writing slants expresses the writer's approach to other people. One can use a protractor for this purpose. The central upright 90 degree angle is the stance taken by people who are conventional, self-confident and calm. They may give the impression of being aloof because, although they have emotions, they keep them well in check. Diplomats are often found to have this upright style of writing.

When the writing leans to the left, the writer is shy and often uncommunicative He is usually very cautious and does not take easily to the idea of change. He is concerned more with the past in his life, with family and tends to be conservative in his outlook.

Conversely, the right-sloping writing is an indication of a more extrovert nature. This writer is more outgoing, less inhibited and is good at personal relationships.

It is sometimes said that if two strangers are alone at a bus stop, the extrovert is the one who speaks first! The extrovert is a gregarious, often affectionate person who is more interested in other people and the future than his more introverted, cautious, backward looking counterpart.

However, as with every other form of indication, these tendencies must be taken into account with other factors and it is combinations of all of these that give us an insight into people's characters.

Now and again

The inhibited, cautious introvert

Now and again

The sociable, demonstrative extrovert

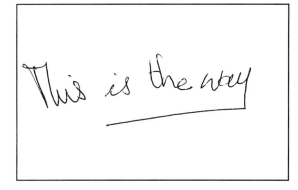

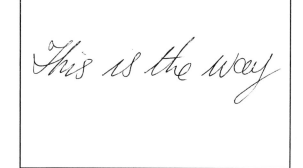

The upright form of the person
who writes in two ways

The forward form of the person
who writes in two ways

A person may find himself writing in two ways, upright and to the right. He is versatile, being more reserved and wary of strangers but quite sociable with the people he knows.

Others write with a left and right slant at one and the same time. This type of writing usually stems from insecurity and a lack of self-confidence, stemming from a poor educational background. The writer is never quite sure of his ground.

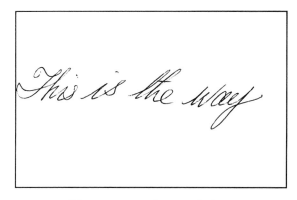

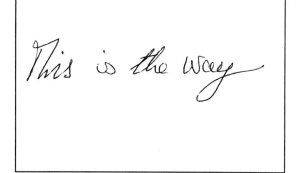

A mixed hand, more left than right

A mixed hand, more right than left

The greater angle of slant denotes a corresponding degree of introversion or extroversion. In fact, anyone whose writing comes within 10 or even 20 degrees to the left or 10 to 20 degrees to the right comes within the norm. However, occasionally one observes a wider angle and here we find the more extreme nature. If to the right the person is intensely emotional, even hysterical. If very much to the left, and this is rare, the person is extremely shy and painfully self-conscious, even isolated.

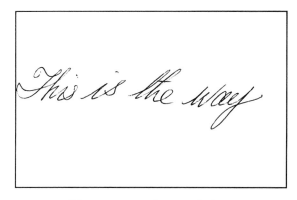

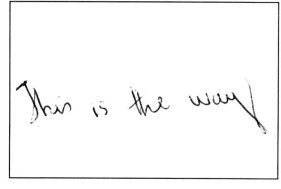

The extreme forward slant

The extreme backward slant

The Three Zones

Graphologists divide handwriting into three zones and they all tell us a great deal about the personality of the writer.

The Upper Zone

The Middle Zone

The Lower Zone

The upper zone reveals the spiritual side of our life, to what extent we reach up to higher ideals. It is, if you like, our head in the sky. If it is of normal size, ie, twice the size of the middle letters, this is fine, but if it is larger then we have a fantisiser, an idealist

The middle zone shows our heart line, the one we use for every day. People whose middle letters are proportionately larger than the upper or lower loops live for today and are not particularly intellectual or interested in the physical side of life.

The lower zone indicates our feet on the ground. People who have large lower loops have a strong sense of materialism and may be a lover of possessions.

The writer of the above example was an RAF Padre, a very strong-minded character with high spiritual ideals as can be seen by the high upper loops, especially in his capitals. The lower loops reflect his love of sport. It is interesting to note the semi-Roman style in which he wrote the date. Sadly the writing is not very legible, in the same way that we sometimes found his sermons to be a little 'above our heads'!

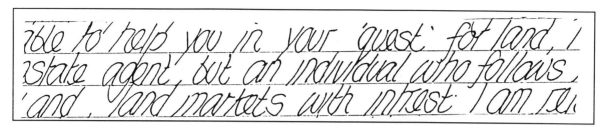

Middle letters dominate the scene - an egocentric

Where the middle letters dominate the scene, the writer is not particularly intellectual nor yet again especially interested in physical matters. He is here for today and for himself only, an egocentric.

29.7.84

Dear Angela & Bob,

Thank you very much for a lovely party, I did enjoy myself. You had arranged everything so beautifully with the delicious refreshments, pretty surroundings and happy

The artistic hand of a lady who was a musician and a potter

Lower loops show the physical side of our lives, whether, for instance, we play a musical instrument and make pottery as the lady who wrote the graceful example given above.

Pen Pressure

The type of pressure created by a writer gives us further clues as to his nature.

People who press heavily upon the paper, producing a Braille effect on the reverse of the sheet, tend to be strong, robust and physically fit. Sometimes the words will be impressed as far down as two or three pages of 80 gram paper. This sort of person usually prefers to be out of doors, often they are athletic They are not the contemplative sort, they prefer action to sitting around. Frequently they are possessive and take pride in their strong sense of sight, smell, taste, etc. They enjoy working with their hands and are proud of what they do. Often heavy pressure is accompanied by the use of a broad nibbed pen. It is also found in the script of those who are rather emotionally insecure and therefore have a short fuse as a form of defence. Such people 'fly off the handle' at any indication of criticism and tend to forestall someone who is taking the initiative and might put them in the wrong.

Reversely, the person who creates no impression on the back of the paper and whose writing is thin and delicate are usually more sensitive. They tend to choose a pen with a fine point and are often artistic. It is important when thinking of pen pressure to observe the slant of the writing and to take other factors into account.

Most people write with a medium pressure, so that the impression on 80 gram paper is only just discernible. These types of people come from all walks of life and are as interested in doing as in just thinking. They like doing physical tasks but are also happy to sit around for part of their lives, reading or watching television. They are not fussy as to the type of pen nib they use and may be just as happy with a ballpoint.

Other types of pressure include pasty, which is comprised of a flat and even stroke, with little or no sign on the back of the page and indicates sensory response and a good visual memory.

Where the pressure is uneven, some parts of the writing being detectable on the reverse and some not, this can be a danger sign regarding personal equanimity and control. It can be a negative feature in a low quality script.

Heavy pen pressure

Pasty pen pressure

Medium pen pressure

Uneven pen pressure

Light pen pressure

Size of Writing

The size of a person's handwriting shows us how the writer perceives the world around him and where he makes his place in it.

Large writing belongs to the very active person who sees the world as a whole, a big thinker and mover. He is well travelled and takes an interest in many things at once - many people in the entertainment field have large writing. For this type of person a 24 hour day is simply not enough!

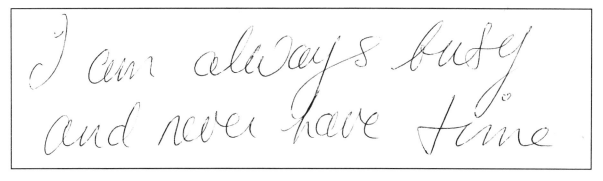

Large sized writing

Medium writing is that done by most people and therefore you will have to be especially careful to look at all other aspects of the script. Quite often an individual may write in a medium size, but when he becomes extra busy his handwriting increases in size. One would think that smaller writing, taking up less space, would be easier for him, but it is actually quicker to dash off large writing!

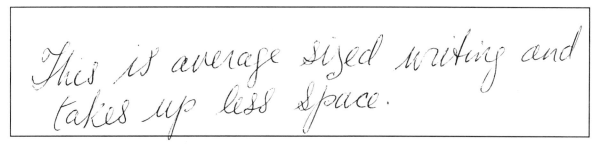

Average sized writing

Small writing shows a hermit-like character, usually a person who lives alone or with someone who is understanding of their need to be left alone for long periods, perhaps to study or just to enjoy peace and quiet! They cultivate just a few friends and usually keep them for many years. These people are very determined, concentrate on what they plan to do and achieve their ends with the minimum of effort.

Small writing

Miniscule writing

Capital Letters

We can perceive a great deal from the way in which a writer makes his capitals. They give clues as to whether he is proud and egotistical or modest and humble.

On the whole, the larger his capitals, the greater a person's pride in himself and his achievements. However, the writer of small capitals is one who has no great ambition and is quite happy with the situation in which he finds himself. What is important when studying capitals is to relate them to the rest of the word and, indeed, to the remainder of the sentence.

Old-fashioned capitals

Capitals that have taken a very ornate form are those made by people who are old-fashioned and proud of it. They value what they see as traditional old-world values where social graces were held in high esteem.

Square cut capitals show a constructive ability and those which are of Roman design indicate a person used to exercising his authority.

Square-cut capitals

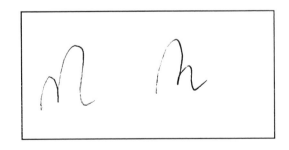

Flamboyant capitals

As we saw in the chapter on the Three Zones, large upper loops show flamboyance and this is particularly true of capital letters, especially the L, the P and the R.

The capital M in particular will reveal a person's attitude towards others. If the first part of the M is lower than the second, the writer puts others before himself and where the reverse applies, he thinks of himself first.

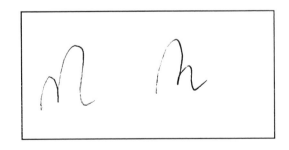

Capital M referred to on the left

Over ornate capitals

Large and over-ornate capitals betray vulgarity and tell us that the writer has a taste for ostentation.

Where the capitals are only a little larger than the main writing, the person has little ambition or need to show off his abilities. He is content to occupy his allotted place in life.

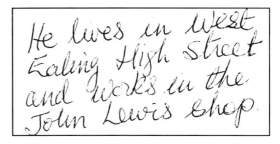

Small capitals

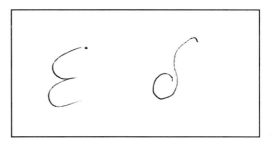

Tall, narrow capitals

Tall, narrow capitals tend to be written by people who are ambitious but are, at the same time, tense and inhibited. They often fail to meet their ultimate goal.

The Greek form of capital E, especially when accompanied by the same form of the lower case 'd' reveals private education and a comfortable home background.

Greek E and lower case 'd'

Sometimes you come across capitals in the middle of the sentence, where they are really not necessary. This style was much in use in Georgian and Victorian times, but seen in a modern hand, the writer is pedantic and over-fussy, perhaps prone to rebellion. However, in Ireland the use of the capital R, not only at the start of the sentence but in any place within the script, is taught in schools, probably for the sake of clarity.

Pedantic handwriting

't' Bars and 'i' Dots

It is surprising how much can be derived from a study of these parts of two single lower case letters. In fact, you will probably be amazed how many different versions of them occur, often differing ones in the same document. It has been estimated that there are over fifty different types!

The horizontal stroke of the 't' bar shows the amount of force and willpower exerted by the individual and reveals a great deal about how he reacts in a crisis.

When the cross on the 't' is central, we know that the writer is conventional, it is the form he was taught at school. This person conforms to the rule but may not be very adaptable.

Where the cross is longer and away from the upright we see enthusiasm and, if the bar is also sloping upwards, this is accompanied by a cheerful disposition.

If the bar is downwards, however, there may be unhappiness and a reluctance to give in gracefully.

Sometimes a hooked cross bar is observed. The writer is tenacious, reluctant to leave the paper. He hangs on to his purpose and has a great deal of energy.

The looped 't' bar shows persistence and is often used as a short form to facilitate speed.

A bow-shaped bar, especially one made over the top of the upright, is a sign of beneficence. It reveals a lofty imagination, one who aspires spiritually. It is often found in the writing of clergymen and charitably minded people.

A 't' bar that is bowed in a concave manner is the opposite of the one that is bowed in a convex way. That is to say, the writer often comes down hard on those nearest to him, especially if they are in a weaker position.

Where the bar is downwards and heavy, like a club, we see aggressive and unpredictable behaviour.

Sometimes you observe a 't' bar that goes from the left of the stem. If it starts there and does not touch the upright, the writer often starts things and does not finish them. He tends to procrastinate and is often lacking in self-confidence.

The elongated 't' bar shows a caring disposition. If it is straight then the writer's advice will have to be taken, but if more soft, kindness is shown.

A 'fly-away' 't' bar is a sign of impatience and impetuosity, it reveals enthusiasm and an urgency to get on with the task in hand.

Where the bar is close to the upright, we see signs of repression, and often guilt.

If the 't' bar runs straight across, but above the upright, we are dealing with a person who is reaching for the unattainable, a fantasy world.

A wavy 't' bar shows a sense of humour, adaptability and a warm nature.

Where the bar is straight up it denotes ambition, accompanied by optimism. This person will get his own way but in a pleasing manner.

In all of the above cases, and there are many, many more, they are frequently accompanied by the same form of 'i' dot. When you come to analyse writing for yourself you should look to see how many times the characteristic occurs and whether there are variables. Consistency confirms a type, inconsistency means that the writer is more flexible. In all cases they reveal much about the temperament of the writer.

Again, as in the 't' bar, the person who places the 'i' dot exactly above the stem is one who conforms to the rule and tends not to be very adaptable.

The high 'i' dot shows imagination and lofty ideals. It is usually found along with the 't' bar that is above the stem.

Where the dot has a hook to it, rather like a tent, it indicates a critical nature. It is usually found in angular writing.

The 'i' dot that is behind the upright is quite common. It shows caution and may be seen with a corroborating 't' bar which remains on the left of the stem.

The circle type of dot reveals individuality in the writer, usually a sense of humour but certainly a need to be seen to be different from other people.

The Personal Pronoun

The capital 'I', the personal pronoun, has great significance for it gives clues to the personality of the writer not revealed in other letters. It shows us how the writer sees himself, whether his self-esteem is high or low.

Quite often the personal pronoun will be written in a different manner from other capital 'I's and this shows certain inner qualities of the writer even more clearly.

Where several forms of the personal pronoun are used within one document, it is a sign that the writer is adaptable but may also be unpredictable.

If the personal pronoun is much larger than the other capitals, we see an egotistical writer, one who has a high opinion of himself.

The person who makes a single, tall, upright stroke to represent himself is one who has a highly developed intellect, usually accompanied by a private education. He does not fuss over what he sees as trivialities. Such personal pronouns are often accompanied by single strokes instead of loops on the small 'h', 'k' and 'l'.

Where this type of formation is shorter, the ego is still firm and again it shows that the writer comes down to basic details very quickly. However, he may not be quite so confident as the writer of the tall version.

The capital formed like a Roman numeral shows clear thinking but a form of severity too, it indicates a business-like approach. The top and bottom bars act rather like tramlines, keeping the writer within set tracks.

This capital 'I' has a little cap on it and reveals a person who thinks a great deal but gives very little away.

The looped, scripted version shows emotion, but it is kept in check.

The fuller form shows a more sociable and outgoing writer.

The closer, tighter version, on the other hand, shows tension.

A similar style, but more angled is made by the aggressive, self-righteous writer.

Spaces Between Lines and Words

The space between the lines of writing and the space between the words themselves are an indication of how the writer reacts to other people. Basically there are three forms: the one we are taught at school, enough distance between the lines to prevent confusion and enough distance between the words to make each one distinct.

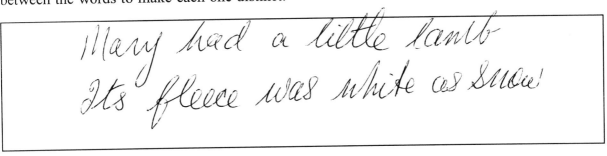

The well organised hand where the upper and lower loops do not touch.

The second is where the writer mixes the upper and lower loops, usually through a lack of forethought and organisation. Such people are often frantically busy but actually waste time because they can't find things!

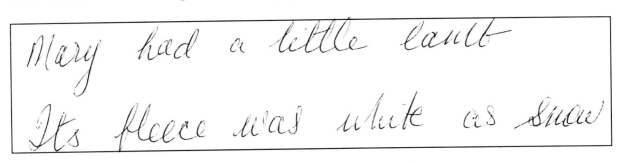

Confused line spacing, accompanied by words close together

The third type is quite different. Here the writer separates the lines to such an extent that it is quickly obvious that he prefers to choose the company he keeps! Such writers also tend to separate their words more than is normal and the more this is exaggerated, the more isolated they have become. When accompanied by an upright hand, the person may seem very aloof.

Both lines and words are set wide apart from one another

How Words are Joined

Graphologists divide the manner in which words are connected into four main groups: Garland, Arcade, Angle and Thread. At first these are not obvious, but when you have been studying this subject for some time you will easily be able to distinguish one from the other.

The garland is a sociable script and most often used by females because it is the easiest and allows the down stroke to be connected to the following up stroke in a flowing movement from left to right. Garland writers tend to take the path of least resistance and are often open to outside influences.

Garland writing

The arcade, often a copybook style, is made in the reverse manner. The curves are closed towards the upper zone and open towards the lower zone. People who write like this are reserved and tend to be rather formal in their dealings with people they do not know well. They are often sensitive and have a good memory for small details.

Arcade writing

Angled writing, often a masculine trait, is full of spikes and often represents an unwillingness to conform and adapt. People who write in an angular manner prefer difficulty to smoothness. They are usually strictly ethical and like a challenge. They are determined people, often strongly motivated and very sincere. The writer of this sample, which shows some angularity, is a retired schoolmaster.

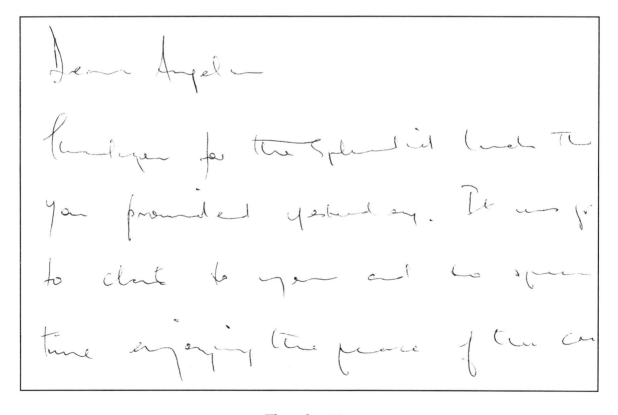

Angled writing

Thread writers usually have an attractive personality and like to be able change their minds. Theirs is a fluid way of life, and they are often very creative. They are quick to take advantage of an opportunity but tend to avoid convention. They are broad minded and agile thinkers. However, they are usually very short of time and use short forms to make up for this.

Thread writing

Interpreting Signatures

Many people sign their names in a script that matches the body of the letter. In this case the interpretation of the signature is relatively easy, but many writers like to make an individual mark, one that says: "This is me and no-one else." This may be a guard against forgery, though forgers, who turn the original around in many ways before they make their copy, will often succeed in fooling all but the expert!

It is very unwise to try and make even the most superficial of comments on seeing the signature alone. It needs to be viewed along with the main text where often a great difference will be noticed between the two and this itself is significant.

Apart from general interest, there is little point in the amateur studying the signatures of television personalities or film stars, because these people have developed a flamboyant style to match their lifestyles. Often their writing before they became famous was much smaller and neater. Some signatures of people in the entertainment world are quite amusing, a few have even adapted their name to their vocation, ie where the capital P becomes a grand piano!

Much better to concentrate on the people you know, so you can put what you are learning with what you already know about them. If the signature is very unusual, you may even be able to ask them how and why they came to do it in this way.

A person's signature often changes as he matures and it is interesting to be able to gather examples from members of one's own family to show how this has happened.

Where the structure of the signature remains the same throughout life, you can be sure that this is also true of the person themselves, but many people change enormously throughout their lives, especially where they have become very successful in a particular field.

So let us examine a few specimens and see how they relate to the body of the text as well.

Where the signature is much larger than the text, the writer thinks of himself as being important and wishes to stand out in society, to be a big fish in a small pond.

On the other hand, where the signature is smaller than the text, the writer is modest, humble and has a low opinion of himself. He tends to hide away - this style is often found with the backward sloping writing of the shy individual.

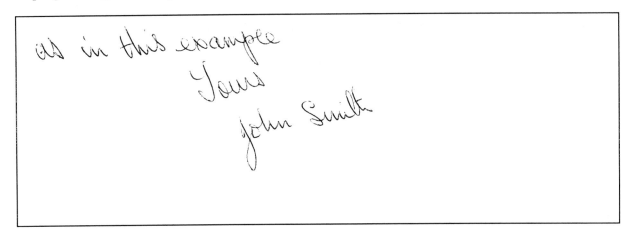

Where the signature is legible, you find honesty, a respect for the law and a wish to achieve clarity.

Where the signature is not clear, but the name is printed or typed underneath, the writer is still honest but may have developed an illegible signature after say, years of signing documents.

You may discover instances where the clarity in the first and second names varies. This will arise from the writer's opinions of himself and of his family or, in the case of a woman, her husband's family. In the next example, the writer thinks highly of himself, but has a poor opinion of his father or his father's family. He might want to exert his independence.

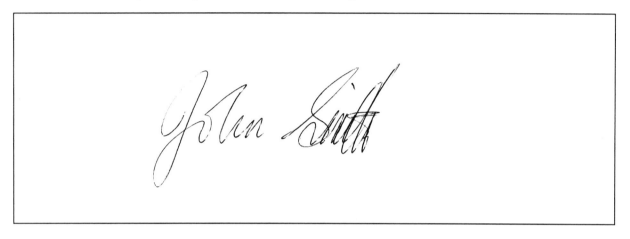

Here the family name is important, but the writer himself believes he doesn't match up to this level.

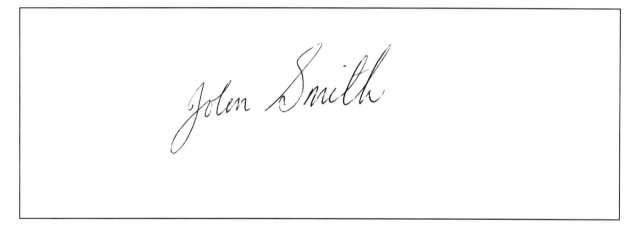

Where the signature is highly embellished, there is pride, self-respect and a love of show and ostentation. This type of writer is often 'snobby' and may be one of the 'nouveau riche'.

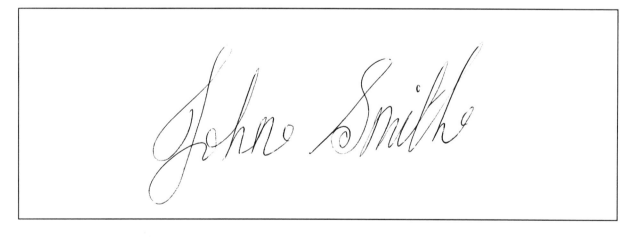

As we saw in the section on the angle of lines, a falling signature, especially where this is not usually the case, shows temporary depression, especially in times of bereavement.

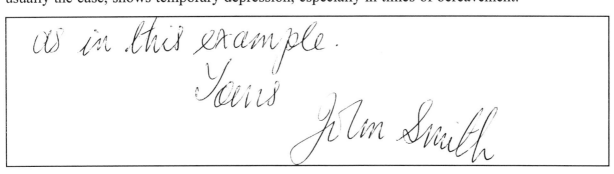

On the other hand, someone who has just won the Lottery might make a much more optimistic, upward slanting signature than they would normally do!

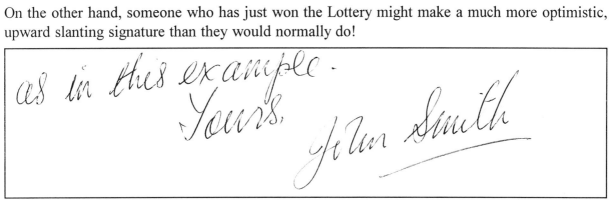

Many people underline their signature. This is for emphasis and the person who does so likes to have his wishes carried out. Where the name is underlined several times this is even more so, although it does also sometimes occur in letters written by busy people who feel they must fill all the space in the same way that they must fill all their time!

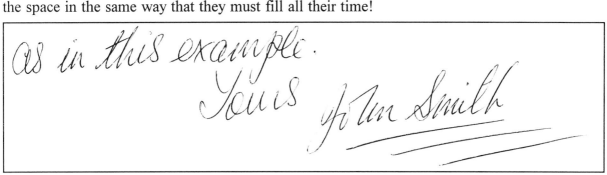

A full stop after the signature is unnecessary and is an indication that the writer has spoken, "and there is an end to it!"

Speed of Writing

The speed with which a person moves can often be judged by his writing. Speed can be accomplished by writing large, using short forms or by joining words together.

In the example below, the writer has joined firstly four words and then three words, without taking his pen off the paper. He is obviously a man who thinks fast on his feet!

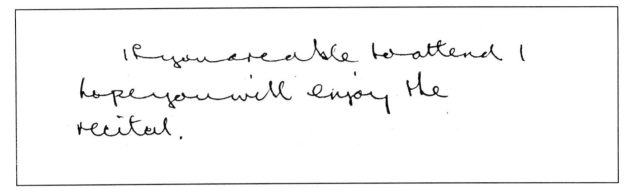

This person writes at normal speed. Although there are breaks in the joining of the letters, they are linked where the writer feels it looks elegant enough to do so.

This hand is much slower. The writing is carefully formed in a traditional, copybook style. The writer is older and takes more time to write clearly and legibly.

A Few Last Pointers

When you are analysing your correspondence, a number of other factors will also strike you, for instance, what type of paper is used and what type and colour of pen? All of these components, together with your new-found knowledge of graphology, will help you to make an assessment.

Unlike the earlier days of the twentieth century, when middle and upper class people had time on their hands and prided themselves on their handwriting, unfortunately today electronic mail is tending to replace the letter, as has the telephone call. Nevertheless, people do like to receive letters, especially in times of bereavement, and there is no doubt that they are a comfort, for they can be read over and over again.

Therefore even people who use e-mail do still write letters and keep notepaper for that purpose. Usually the notepaper is the same as the writer has always used and the type of it will reveal something about the writer. Good quality, A5 size, cream or pale grey, with the address already printed at the top and with its own matching envelopes is preferred by people of good taste.

Pastel colours, such as pink or blue, are favoured by women, and in the artistic this may run to a Florentine style border and envelope with matching interior. Fortunately, scented notepaper seems to have gone out of fashion, chiefly because when the perfume faded on the shop shelf, it became less pleasant! Teenage girls often choose, (or are given!) stationery with floral motifs or animal illustrations.

My experience, however, is that men prefer a sheet of A4 paper, of good weight, such as Conqueror, together with matching side-opening 9" x 4" envelope.

The choice of pen is also very indicative as to the nature of the writer. Bold people prefer thicker pens, sometimes even resorting to felt tips, though these may make the writing difficult to read. The broad nib of a fountain pen is usually preferred and I am always amused when lecturing to watch the reaction of the audience when I state: "People of character use a fountain pen." Smiles and nods of acknowledgement are soon forthcoming until I say: "But I didn't say whether they were of good or bad character!" However, there is no doubt that a fountain pen does create a good impression, as it gives a variable outline to the lettering, though there is a nuisance factor in having to refill it. Nevertheless it is far better than a ball-point, which often smudges. Perhaps the best compromise is the roller ball, like the Papermate. The calligraphic pen, along with Indian ink, is sometimes used by people who have an artistic flair and have done a course in this type of lettering. It is very pleasing and may replace their less legible handwriting.

Most men prefer to use black or blue/black ink, which looks business-like and clear. Women like blue - it is a colour associated with seriousness and reliability, whilst at the same time not being as hard as black. Red ink has never been favoured for correspondence. Traditionally, blood was used to write threatening letters, like those sent by 'Captain Swing' in the days of the agricultural riots. People who write in green or turquoise ink like to be noticed and are often artistic. Purple ink is rarer but, again, it is a sign of an artistic, even flamboyant nature, especially where the writing and signature are large.

Understanding Your Family

After reading through all these rules, you may well be asking yourself "How and when can I make use of all I have learned?" The answer is "Easily, here and now!"

We will start by analysing the writings of a family. As examples, I have used those of my own. I am often asked about compatability and opposite are two clear examples, those of my mother and father. They lived and worked together happily for over 60 years. The reason for this can be seen in the fact that they both wrote with a forward slope, always going ahead and looking to the future.

My father's writing leans slightly less to the right and is more angular - he was very good at figures. His narrow margins reflect his greater care for money and this balanced my mother's ability to spend it. My father had few loops in his writing, he was very much a practical man and the underscore he placed below his name showed that he expected his wishes to be carried out!

My mother's writing is very rounded and affectionate, with the upper and lower loops of the more emotional person. The margin is wide, a sign of generosity and it widens as she progresses through this note - a sign that she was less sure of herself at first and then became happier with what she was trying to convey. It is well formed and as perfect as she could make it, which was typical of her attitude towards life - everything had to be orderly and of the best quality she could afford. Her 'fly-away' type 't' bars and 'i' dots show impatience and a need to have everything immediately.

My father's handwriting when he was about 50 years of age

My mother's handwriting when she was about 50 years of age

In later life my mother's beautiful writing has deteriorated somewhat, due to arthritis in her hands and the ageing process generally. However, the structure can still be seen clearly, as in the example below. Note the sharp rise in the level of the lines, as she tries to be cheerful in face of adversity. Also that the 'i' dots and 't' bars have, to a large extent, come back from the speedy 'fly-away' style to a more normal position. It has also become more upright, as she learns to live for today.

My mother's handwriting when she was over 90 years of age

However, the fact that both parties' handwriting slopes the same way is not a necessary factor in a happy relationship. When my husband and I met about fifty years ago, our handwritings were very different.

It was not until I started to take an interest in graphology that I noticed, even after about ten years of marriage, our angles were still quite wide apart. At that time I kept a copy of a letter he had written and wrote the same words myself in the space below.

You will note that Bob's writing is backward leaning but strong. Even at that time he created a Braille effect on the reverse side of the paper. The backward slant reveals his innate sense of caution and his suspicion of anything new.

His fully crossed 't' bars show determination, self-discipline and attention to detail - vital qualities for the qualified engineer. In the word 'the' before 'trouble' the 't' bar takes on a hook, revealing tenacity of purpose, what he proudly calls 'stickability'!

Some of his upper and lower loops are full, but most of them are straight - a combination of some emotion but mostly a dispensing with what he sees as unnecessary frivolities.

The 'W' that begins the second paragraph denotes a leaning backward towards the past and a father figure. Bob has often looked back on his childhood with happy memories and thought very highly of his father, looking upon him as a role model.

The capitals are exactly twice the size of the middle letters. In this young man there was little ambition, he was quite happy in a middle management position and was good at his job.

My writing of exactly the same words could hardly be more different. At that time, a young mother with a part-time job, I was always quick off the mark.

The angle of my writing shows the same forward leaning, forward looking attitude as my parents had and the impatience and impetuosity that you can observe in my mother's writing. People say we look alike, so it is not surprising that we write in a similar manner! However, mine is a much less carefully formed hand than that of my mother.

The writing is large, a sign of a busy person with a wide field of interests. Whereas my husband's lines are straight and show great method and order, mine were, and still are, inclined to rise in a cheerful and optimistic manner.

My 't' bars are angled upwards, too and though most of the 'i' dots are roughly above the stem, several of them fly impatiently away to the right.

Almost all my upper and lower loops are full, though a few show the tightness that comes with the stress and tension of balancing a job with a housewifely life.

Above all, this writing shows a need for speed. I was able to type far faster than I could write and my learning of shorthand gave me a taste for short-forms to enable me to write faster. Examples of this can be seen in the 'g' of 'given' and in the 't' at the end of 'account'.

Thank you for your letter of the 27th October and taking the trouble to us on all the various aspects of Michael's progress at School.

We are pleased that he ha settled down and given quite a good account of himself in most direction

My husband's handwriting at about 35 years of age

Thank you for your letter of 27 October and taking the trouble advise us on all the various a of Michael's progress at School.

We are pleased that he has sett down and given quite a good ac

My own writing at about 35 years of age

When our nephew was about twelve, I had recently taken up graphology and was able to use my new found skills to help him in a small way.

On receiving a letter of thanks for a birthday gift when he was 14, I noticed, by drawing lines at right-angles to the edge of the notepaper, that his handwriting was sloping downwards. I did not remember it happening so markedly before and so spoke to my sister-in-law about my anxieties. She confirmed that he had been doing a lot of extra-mural activities, including scouting.

A few weeks later Adrian was able to relinquish some of these activities and his next letter, (shown opposite) received about three months afterwards, showed a remarkable improvement.

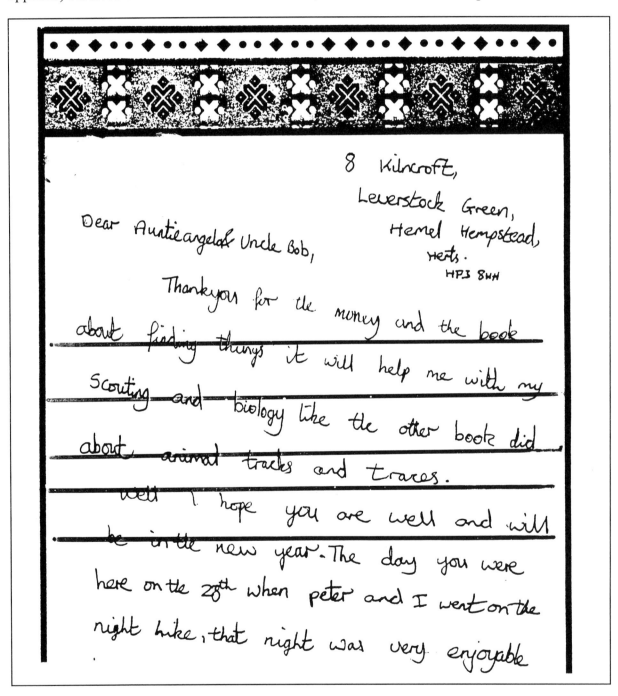

To Auntie Angela & Uncle Bob,

Thankyou for having us
for the weekend, it was very
enjoyable. I enjoyed myself
alot, especially making the
Bonfires and going to child Beale.
The meals were excellent and
I loved them. I see whats the
difference is between wild
rabbits and tame rabbits because
my freind has got some

In this letter, the lines of Adrian's handwriting had become significantly straighter.

Adrian was a quiet little boy, with average writing for his age and the small capitals that show no great ambition, just a contentment with life as it is. He is now more mature and has a worthwhile job that he enjoys, but basically he is still the same. His younger brother, Peter, however, was quite different and one of his letters, written when he was 12, is shown opposite. He was, and to some extent still is, an artistic person, with a flair for doing the unexpected. His tendency to be eye-catching at that particular age is not only revealed in the drawings but also in the fact that it was written in red ink! His 'i' dots reveal his sense of humour and his hooked lower loops reveal a tenacity that he still has. The hook on his capital 'T's also shows persistence and this has been confirmed in his later life. He is still very warm, demonstrative and generous, but has sobered down considerably since he wrote this letter! He now has a very good job in computing.

I have also been interested to look back on the gradual formation of the writing of their elder sister, Vanessa. Letters written by her in 1980, when she was 12 and then four years later and thirdly four years later again when she was a student show fascinating growth in her self-confidence from a little girl to a maturing young woman. She is now happily married with a baby son.

It was in her student days that she developed the long 't' bar with its tenacious hook. It shows that she benificently cares for others and happily plans future projects and then carries them through with tenacity. As her aunt, who has watched her grow up, I can confirm the truth of these indications.

Dear Auntie Angela and
Uncle Bob

Thankyou for the lovely time we spent with you on Sunday and Monday. Fiona and I enjoyed the meals and Fiona thought

Many thanks for the money which I'm sure you know is always gratefully recieved by all poor penniless teenagers. I'd also like to add how much I enjoyed Christmas Eve; especially playing consequences which always proves to be amusing with Grandad's corny

Thanks for the cheque — Amazingly enough it has found its way rather pronto into the "European holidays for students" fund. The route is now Paris — 'the south' —

Thanks A lot AA. & UB.

(After You)
(Have Finished)
(P.T.O.)

8 Kilncroft
Leverstock Green
Hemel Hempstead
Hants
HP3 8HH

P.No 3014

To
Dear
Auntie
Angela & Uncle Bob,

Thanks Very Much, for letting us stay at the Old Place.

I really enjoyed it and especially at Chilbeak. Hope you keep the garden in full shape, Hope you are well, Lots Of love Peter

XX

Writing this book has prompted me to look back at the way in which our two sons' writing changed from when they first went to boarding school to when they were at university. As they both went to the same preparatory school it is not surprising that their writing styles were not dissimilar in the days when they had just arrived at Berkhamsted. However, even at that age, Philip's lower loops were straight, whereas Michael's were more full. Philip has always been one to get straight down to matters - Michael will chat a bit at first. Both the boys used the single stroke form of the personal pronoun - a form unanimously agreed by graphologists to be intelligent, masculine, natural, cultured but unaffected.

Philip, aged 13

Michael, aged 13

The next two examples show the handwriting of both our sons when they were at university. By this time Philip's writing had developed the style he still has. He continued to use the single upright form of the personal pronoun, but his lower and upper loops have developed as he has become more mature. The lines of both boys' writing, which decended slightly in his early letters from boarding school, have taken on a level, even slightly upward slope. At this time Philip was starting work on his PhD in Astrophysics at Imperial College, London and his smaller writing reflects the narrowing of his field. I noted at this time that his pedantic style of writing began to strongly resemble that of Bob's eldest sister, who was also an academic. An interesting point here for those fascinated by genetics, neither of their writings resembled mine or that of my husband!

Michael's writing, on the other hand, had begun to resemble that of my brother. It was rounded and affectionate, with small capitals that indicated no great ambitions or flamboyancy. However it had taken on a certain amount of angle - he was beginning to rebel against what he saw as any unnecessary restrictions on his lifestyle! There is also a certain amount of falling off at the end of the lines and other indications of carelessness and a general happy-go-lucky attitude that he still has.

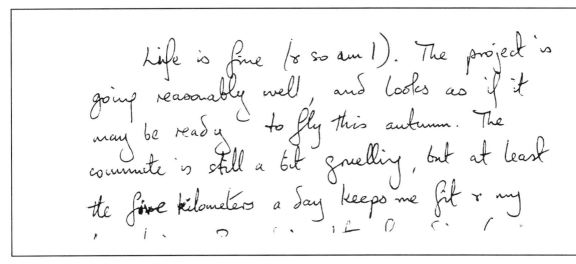

Philip's writing at 22

Michael's writing at 20

Learning more about Your Friends

One of the oldest letters in my collection is one we received from an elderly lady who had been our 'baby-sitter' when our sons were young. I had often admired her delightful handwriting and the excellent way in which she expressed herself, even though she had only been educated in a village school in Warwickshire.

We continued to correspond long after the boys had grown up and her letters were still beautifully written.

It was a great shock, therefore, to receive the following communication from her in which the writing is very angular, uneven and generally unstable, although the old optimism still showed in the rising lines. Not only was the handwriting very shaky, but the contents were rambling and I realised at once that something was dreadfully wrong. A telephone call to her son soon revealed that she had recently suffered a stroke, although she herself did not mention it in the letter, which was actually the left-hand side of a Christmas card. Sadly, she died soon afterwards.

One of our much-loved friends is renowned for her scatty, extrovert manner. She is a very natural person, who speaks in short sharp runs and places emphasis on what she feels to be the most important words. Her angular style handwriting reflects all these qualities.

However, much of this zaniness is just a facade, born of a nervous energy. She is actually a very sincere, caring person, as witnessed by the 't' bars, which go over the tops of three and even four letters. Her concern for others is a part of her deep Christian commitment and the love that she shows to everyone, revealed in the fullness of her 'a's and 'o's, although tension can be seen in the tightness of some of the 'e's.

Her large writing shows her love of travel, her broad overview of life. Her passion for adventure can be seen in the irregularity of the writing and the unevenness of the lines reveals her ability to adapt to the many strange situations in which she finds herself in foreign countries.

I'd like to share one of my experiences of God: –
My friend told how he was desperate to know God's
will. He went into the church to pray "Lord! is
my girlfriend the one you want me to marry. I
want to marry her but what's your will?" –
Immediately a lady who he didn't know, came from
the back of the church. She said, "God, has told
me to tell you to read psalm 45. I don't know why
but its a message from God". He went home and
read the psalm. A complete confirmation that
he should marry his girl friend. Psalm 45 is
about a Royal Wedding!!
   The following morning, I was traveling home
from Mass in the bus, along the highway (sometimes
it went along the back roads) I told the passenger
my friends story. I got off the bus and walked past
a hedge. Behind the hedge sat a Filipino girl. As I
told her the story I picked the leaves off the hedge.
I got home and thought, "Lord am I doing alright?" I
picked up my Bible and the 1st words I read were: –
"Go out to the highways and hedges and compel people
to come in" Luke 14 verse 23. Thank you Lord for speaking
to me too!

- 39 -

The example opposite is that of a very good friend who has considerable intellectual faculties and a wicked sense of humour! As can be seen from the opening greeting, he has a flair for puns. This one was based on his having just discovered that my husband had bought a Space Wagon, which he finds easy to get in and out of because he is tall and long-legged ("like my favourite animal, the giraffe") and that I had just started to write this book on graphology! His tall upright letters show great intelligence and also stability. His 'o's, which are closed tightly at the base, reveal his ability to keep a secret, which is very important, as he is a Registrar. He admitted to doing two forms of handwriting, the printed version at the top, carefully constructed for entries into registers and his more personal and fluid version lower down. The first part is his business self and the second half is his real, sociable, extrovert counterpart.

We have quite a number of friends in other countries and although 'Christmas letters' are often maligned, we send them and love to receive them, too. I prefer those which, like mine, have a personal note in a space left at the end, and they do help us all to keep in touch, year after year.

One couple that we hear from regularly are Dick and Marilyn who live in New England. Marilyn is a very active, cheerful person whose writing is warm, rounded and affectionate. The most attractive aspect of her letters is that they are very natural - she writes as she speaks. Several of the words are underlined, giving emphasis to those words which she would stress in her speech. Also I love the quirky little sad and happy faces that she draws all over her letters, to echo what she is feeling at that time, in the same way that she 'pulls a face' or grins broadly when she speaks to you! Hers is very much a garland form, but some angular writing is mixed in with it, demonstrating a sharp head with a soft heart!

23rd Sptod 19

Dear Mr & Mrs. Giraffe-Ology,
I have persuaded my tame spider to come out of retirement and crawl along these lines so that you may analyse the little arachnoid. Consequently you may have no fear in analysising the little hairy fellow as he does not appreciate what he is committing to paper.

Many highly esteemed and steamed thanks to you both for an excellent and enjoyable social occasion plus the usual high standard of nosh from who eyes it was in the kitchen. Karin with—. Sorry about that the upright spider is demonstrating fatigue so have substituted one with tired legs hence the tan. We have been out to Didcot and environs today looking for a cabinet all to no avail so have purchased lengths of wood for friendly cripple to assemble

- 41 -

The letter opposite is an interesting one. The original has wide margins on both sides, an indication of culture. The paper used was cream and of excellent quality. The upper loops show a high degree of intellect and self-confidence.

The writing is speedy and some of the fly-away 'i' dots show impatience. The fact that the odd 'i' dot is missing (eg in 'Mill Lane') shows the writer's need to press on with the job in hand.

Most of the 't' bars are those that cross from left to right across the stem, showing caution and an awareness of responsibility. It is the 't' that we were taught to make in school.

The whole letter is well set out, legible and pleasing to the eye. The writer was a wartime pilot, is now a retired schoolmaster and a very active member of the U3A (University of the Third Age).

This rhythmic script is from part of a letter from a very good friend. It is written in green ink, a sign of distinction. People who write in coloured inks tend to be individualists. The large writing is indicative of her busy and active life and her forward flying 'i' dots reveal an impatience to 'get on with things'. Each 't' bar is different, a sign of flexibility. The knotted one in 'to exploring' is a sign of persistence and concentration.

The letter 'f' has a large backward loop - such strokes are indicative of a love of one's family and this large loop shows a pride in their achievements. The full lower loops indicate a physically active person combined with an appreciation of the finer things in life. All the letters are full, revealing the writer's warm and affectionate nature.

The whole is harmonious and attractive, perfectly legible and quite clear. It embodies all the characteristics that I know about the writer.

Dear Angela,

We look forward to hearing your talk on Wednesday March 8th.

The venue is the Oxford Town Football Club Pavilion in Mill Lane, Henley.

We begin our meeting at 2.30 p.m. and I shall be there at 2.p.m. to ensure that all is ready.

We park in the free car park at the end of Mill Lane from which there is a path to the pavilion.

If any problems arise please telephone.

Best wishes,

Sincerely

Frank.

The writer of this letter is a very talented artist, with original ideas. Her arcaded script and Greek 'e's and 'd's show a love of all things beautiful. The graceful curves and large letters show a breadth of vision and the whole is very pleasing to the eye.

This script is certainly individual, but it is clearly legible and written with spontaneity. Her sense of order and her perception of the essentials in a situation can be seen in the regularity of the writing.

Even this short note is well laid out and I was not surprised to find that this lady runs her own graphics design business.

The original of this letter also had wide, cultured margins, but in an effort to retain the original size of the writing, I have had to cut down the margins to fit the space on the page.

Today few people hand write letters except in times of bereavement. However, I have recently published a book, *Dipping into the Wells,* the culmination of twenty years' research into the history of the two villages of Stoke Row and Highmoor in Oxfordshire, on whose boundaries our old cottage stands. In this connection I have been fortunate in receiving a number of kind letters.

The one below was written by a highly respected friend, who was kind enough to read the proofs of that book. His patience in reading and correcting this tome, all 400 pages of it, was very much appreciated and the least I could do was to give him a complementary copy!

His generosity with his time is reflected in his wide left margin and his ability to concentrate for long periods on small details is seen in the smallness of his writing. His personal pronoun is a straight one, no frills here! His capitals are in direct proportion to his middle letters: a man who is quietly capable.

As is witnessed by his 't' bars, most of which stretch over two or even three letters, he is a very caring person. This beneficence is further shown by the slightly curved bar of the capital 'T' for Tony, which also has the slight hook of tenacity which has enabled him to persevere to the end of this mammoth task. The dot after his name is a sign of his having said "And that's it!"

14 : 9 : 99.

Dear Angela,

I am touched by the gift of your book and it's inscription. Believe me, it was a pleasure to watch it mature.

I do admire your persistence. One thing to have the idea — quite another to bring it off in such style.

If Mary's reaction is 'owt to go by, it will go down well. She has been dipping so deep since it came into the house that both wells are more or less dry! My turn next!

Thanks again,

Tony.

Using Graphology in Your Workplace

I spent all my working life in offices, where I was chiefly engaged in sales and marketing administration. As a result, many types of document came into my hands. Sometimes they were just a few words of greetings and signatures on a birthday, get well, or Christmas card, but they were enough to confirm what I had observed in the behaviour of the writer. I soon found my knowledge useful, especially where hiring and firing was concerned.

More often they were letters, memos or other documents and from time to time one caught my eye as being very different from the normal.

Sometimes I was able to be of help to a colleague who had a problem. Below is an example that was sent to me from a friend in publishing with a request for "a few words of advice".

I wrote back: "I think this person has an extremely high opinion of himself as is evidenced by the size of his capitals. He could be said to have his 'head in the clouds' and to be quite unrealistic about everyday life, particularly because the middle letters are so tiny. With such large upper loops, he strikes me as one who is very conceited, arrogant and demanding."

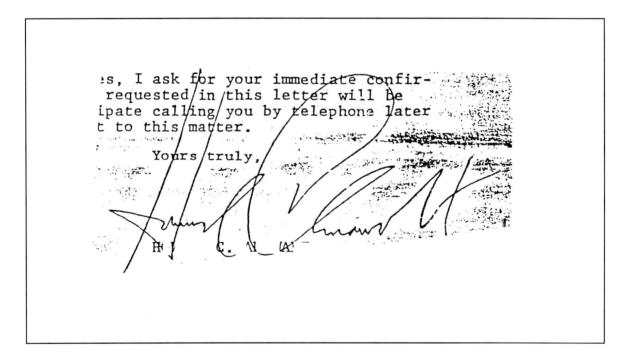

The conceited, arrogant and demanding writer

I was not entirely surprised by the reply I received a few days later: "Thank you. You were quite right. This man threatened to sue my company because he felt he hadn't been given proper credit in a book of his that we published. He did get prime billing in the acknowledgements and appeared in the footnotes, but he wanted his name mentioned in the text too. At the same time the ideas that he wanted credit for were rather minor. I wish we had never taken this author on!"

On another occasion I was handed a memo written in a very strong hand. It had obviously been written with a fountain pen, but, as you may observe, all the cross strokes were very thick and pasty. I instinctively recoiled at the sight of it. and wrote to my boss "The writer of this memo appears to me to be very aggressive and domineering. I see an obstinacy in the heavy manner and think he could be devious." Later, my suspicions were confirmed by other investigations and this tip earned me a large box of delicious chocolates!

Thankfully, few people you meet in offices are like that. The example below was written by a young girl who we employed to feed endless information into a new computer system that had just been installed. Her writing shows a steady type of person, with very little imagination. Fortunately for me, she was quite happy to type boring material into the machine all day. The constant repetition, which would have driven me to drink, did not worry her. "Horses for courses!" was my boss's observation. However, she did have a stubborn side, as can be seen in the regularity of the writing, but it was all relieved by her sense of humour, as indicated by the little circle 'i' dots.

One gentleman I worked for was the Chief Accountant of this organisation - a delightful man who had a very sweet way of pointing out my errors! His hobby was playing the violin, or 'fiddle' as he preferred it called. His sense of rhythm is reflected in the wavy base to his capital 'D's and his executive status is reflected in the Roman form of the capital 'A'. His ability with figures and his critical faculties is seen in his angular writing and his optimism in the upward sloping lines.

I stayed in most of my jobs for long periods, five, seven, ten years, a great deal by today's standards, but I worked for one man for only about a month before I had to give up the job. Had I been able to see his writing before the interview, during which he was really charming, I might not have agreed to work for him in the first place.

As can be seen in the example below, he was a highly intelligent man, but he was very temperamental, domineering and aggressive, sometimes bordering on violent. He shouted a good deal and expected impossible amounts of work to be done in very little time. I had never been afraid of hard work, but I was afraid of him and soon decided I would be happier elsewhere!

For a few months I worked for a car dealership at which there was a young man with a very jolly, extrovert manner. He would bound over the moment a customer came into the showroom and if the situation warranted it, would almost clown about in an effort to demonstrate the latest model. I was confused about this, for his handwriting was that of a shy, unassuming man. My knowledge of graphology naturally made me curious. When I questioned him about the discrepancy between his introverted handwriting and his extroverted behaviour, he admitted ruefully that the latter was a facade that he had developed, because "there's a lot of money to be made by selling cars!"

On another occasion I walked into a room and there on the desk was a memo in a very bold hand, written with a felt tipped pen. It struck me like a thunderbolt and I naturally enquired about the writer. "She's the London boss's secretary and is coming to work here soon!" I was told. I was not surprised that she turned out to be very headstrong, dominant and noisy, slamming filing cabinets and doors. She protected the Chairman like a tiger and saved him many a difficult moment. Actually she was quite likeable and we got on well together, providing I always did as I was asked!

One of the most fascinating aspects of graphology is how everyone's handwriting varies and there is no better time for spotting this than on a greetings card. On the example below there are nearly fifty signatures and each one of them is different! Even a quick study of such a card, backed by your experiences of those people will assist you in getting a picture of the way in which their character matches their handwriting. This example has been reduced to fit the space available.

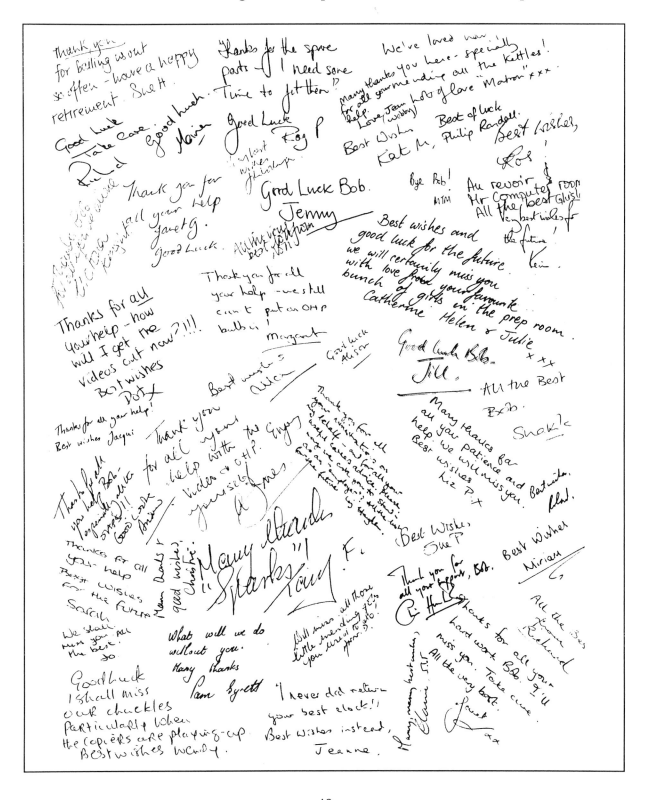

Oodles of Doodles

A doodle is a drawing that we make almost subconsciously, typically during a long and boring telephone call, where the person at the other end of the line is doing all the talking!

Although 'doodles' do not, strictly speaking, come within the sphere of the professional graphologist, they nevertheless do betray our innermost feelings and I am often asked about them. As in handwriting, the sex of the person who makes the marks is not really important, because we all have both masculine and feminine qualities. However, on the whole, men do tend to start out with boxes and women begin with circles. It is what we do with those shapes that reveal our subconscious attitudes and thoughts.

One of the most common forms of doodle is the one which, whether it starts out from a box or a circle, is filled in. The example on the right was done by a student, who was worried about passing her forthcoming exams.

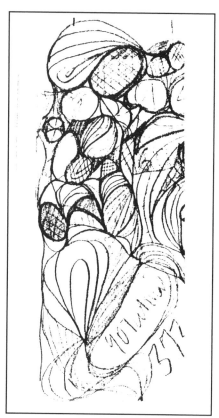

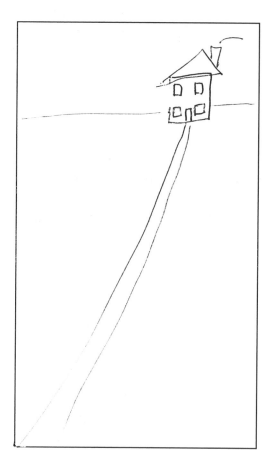

A man will often do a similar type of doodle, but this is based on boxes. In this case the original box becomes his house, the most expensive thing he will ever own - will he be able to keep up the mortgage repayments?!

Women often start out with a circle which then becomes a sun with rays, but this is not a happy vision, it is anxieties shooting out in all directions, looking for solutions!

However, in the lower version the worrier has learned to curb her fears and made them into flowers!

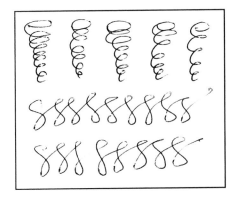

Spirals are another and quite relaxing form of doodle. They start with a ring or an 8, and can go on for as long as we please.

Where a doodle is filled in lightly, the writer is fairly happy, but where the infill is heavy and dark, there may be deep unhappiness, a feeling of inadequacy, an inability to cope.

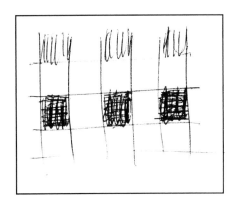

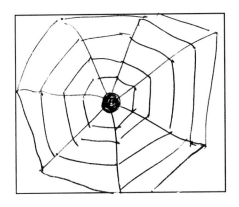

Any doodle with a big black spot is a sign of self-concern. The larger the dot, the bigger the ego. Here the doodler, a salesman with targets to meet, subconsciously imagines himself as the spider waiting to catch an unwary fly.

On a more happy note, faces, animals, hearts and flowers are often doodled by females and show a loving, caring nature.

Making Your Own Analysis

Once you have read through this book and started to collect the handwritings of your friends, family, neighbours and colleagues, you will want to start to make analyses of your own.

Remember that the sex of a person is not necessarily revealed by his/her handwriting. We all have male and female characteristics, it's just that in men the male ones dominate, but one can find females with very masculine qualities and vice-versa. It is the qualities in that person that you are looking for.

Do not be fooled when people say to you "Ah, but I write with my left hand." Sometimes older left-handers were made to write with their right hand at school, but their true nature still shines through. Even people who have been forced by accident or illness to resort to writing and painting with their feet or by holding a pen or brush in their mouth, still show the same qualities.

Even when you are only doing a quick and brief analysis, you must always look for corroborating evidence. Do not just go on one or two clues. Also remember that what you have learned is confidential unless you have the permission of the writer to use it in some way.

Now we come to the actual analysis. To do this you will need a ruler (preferably a transparent plastic one), a protractor, a magnifying glass and a fine red pen.

1. Start by looking at the envelope, if you have one to match the letter. How is the address placed?

2. Once you have opened the letter, note the margins whether they are wide or narrow or a combination of the two. Observe, too, the upper and lower margins.

3. Then you come to the slope of the lines. Do they rise or fall, or are they straight? If they are sloping, to what degree do they do so? Use your ruler at right angles to the edge of the paper, rule underneath with a red pen, so as to make the extent of the slope more clear.

4. Remember to feel the back of the paper, to see if the pressure upon the pen was heavy, or light.

5. Now you begin to look at the writing itself, using your protractor if necessary. Is it upright and stable or does it lean to the left or to the right, or even both ways in the same text?

6. Look closely at the words themselves and note the height and depth of the upper and lower loops. Examine the middle letters, are they full or tight?

7. Is the writing large or small or just average?

8. How are the words connected, is the writing of the Garland, Arcade, Angle or Thread type? This is often not easy to recognise at first, but practice will improve your skills.

9. Observe the capital letters - are they in or out of proportion to the main script? Are they full and generous or tight and tense?

10. Most importantly, note the 't' bars and the 'i' dots. For any of these investigations you may need to use your magnifying glass. If the 't' bars or 'i' dots are occasionally missing, it may indicate carelessness. The number that are not put in will show the depth of that quality. A person who puts in no 't' bars or 'i' dots is rare, one man I know writes a whole paragraph and then goes back and puts in these necessary strokes!

11. Look at how the writer forms his personal pronoun. Is it the straight stroke or a more scripted version?

12. Last of all comes the signature. What can you tell from that?

Make a list of all these points and look up each of them, using this book or, in time, some of the many that you may come to buy. Even though different books contain many varieties of examples, still there may be some that you cannot find, so varied are peoples' handwritings!

From here you should be able to write a short and simple analysis. However, it is very important to realise that, at this stage, you are just a beginner, with perhaps little in the way of psychological knowledge to help you. Nevertheless, you may have been a keen observer of human nature and realise what sort of qualities go together in people and this will assist you in collating your facts.

Bring together all your findings in an orderly manner. You may wish to write your conclusions in a prosaic form or a more business-like one, listing all the qualities one after another. Always state the reasons for your judgement. Then see how these conclusions match what you know about the person - you will be surprised how correct they are!

Always remember to be charitable in your remarks and look for the good in the writer wherever possible. It is quite easy to find euphemistic terms for even the most negative traits, although the stronger ones may need to be pointed out.

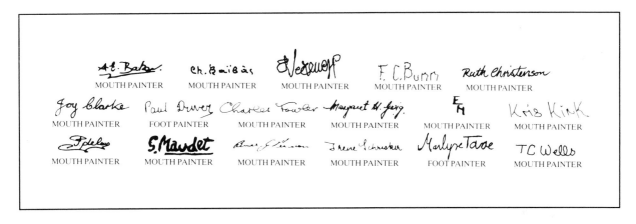

These signatures by the talented members of the Mouth and Foot Painting Artists organisation, MFPA, show how individual their signatures have remained, despite their disabilities.

Conclusion

And so, dear reader, you have reached the last page of this book. I hope it has fired your imagination and given you a taste to find out more. I am sure that by now you will have realised that, without an in-depth study of psychology, and preferably armed with a university degree in the subject, you would not be able to take up this science professionally. However, as an amateur, with constant observation and reading, you will soon learn empirically how to read the characteristics of your family, friends, and colleagues.

Do go on to buy more books. It is quite a good idea to borrow them from your local library first, to see which one suits you. I have listed a few below. If, as a beginner, you were able to buy just one of these, I would recommend Barry Branston's book. Though some may now be out of print, it is often possible to pick them up in second-hand bookshops.

Another way of learning is to go on courses. Early on I attended a seminar given by graphologist Elaine Quigley at Missenden Abbey and found this very instructive. I went to another of Elaine's courses recently at the WI's Denman College and am very grateful to her for reading through the draft of this book for me. Eventually you might like to join the British Institute of Graphologists.

In conclusion, I would like to thank the many people who have given their permission for the inclusion of specimens of their handwriting to be used in this book.

Angela Spencer-Harper
Henley-on-Thames

May, 2000

Title	Author	Publisher	Date
A Manual of Graphology.	Eric Singer.	Gerald Duckworth.	1953
That Doodle Book.	Goodman & Pinkus.	Ocean Books.	1973
Graphology.	Patricia Marne.	Teach Yourself.	1980
A Dictionary of Graphology.	Gloria Hargreaves & Peggy Wilson.	Peter Owen.	1983
What Your Handwriting Reveals.	Margaret Gullan-Whur.	Aquarian Press.	1984
Graphology Explained - A workbook.	Barry Branston.	Piatkus.	1989

A Manual of Graphology. Probably the definitive work, with wonderful drawings by Gertrude Elias.

That Doodle Book. A neat little book, covering many forms of doodle.

Graphology. A handy little book, fits in the pocket.

A Dictionary of Graphology. An excellent work for looking up specific letters and character traits.

What Your Handwriting Reveals. A very clear, concise work, with a very large number of examples.

Graphology Explained - A workbook. An excellent book for the beginner, it is comprehensive, well laid out and very clear.

With the permission of the Parker Pen Company

Notes